Original title:
Through the Pain

Copyright © 2024 Creative Arts Management OÜ
All rights reserved.

Author: Isabella Wilson
ISBN HARDBACK: 978-9908-0-0746-5
ISBN PAPERBACK: 978-9908-0-0747-2

Bonds Forged in Fire

In the kitchen, flames do dance,
We burn the toast, but laugh at chance.
Friends in anguish, food so charred,
We smile and say, this isn't hard!

The goalie missed, the game went south,
We joked instead, and fed our mouth.
A shared misstep, a fumbled play,
Our laughter shines on this sad day.

When We Rise Again

Fell down the stairs, oh what a scene,
My cat just laughed, like a mean machine.
But bruises heal, and so do pride,
We'll dance again, with hope our guide.

A slip on ice, I turned in glee,
Like Bambi lost, yet wild and free.
We rise anew, with every fall,
And find the joy in every sprawl.

Finding Light in the Darkness

The bulb blew out, and darkness fell,
I tripped on shoes—a funny tale to tell.
We fumbled 'round, embraced the night,
With giggles soft, we found our light.

A squirrel stole food, oh what a thief,
We chased him down, no time for grief.
In shadows deep, we found the cheer,
Laughter loud, it chased the fear.

The Language of Suffering

The shoes too tight, what a mistake,
I danced like a fool, my foot did ache.
We shared our woes with wine and cheer,
Turns out, that's how we persevere.

The coffee spilled, an artful mess,
We cracked up hard, I must confess.
In every spill, in every joke,
We find the strength, beneath the smoke.

Heartstrings in Tension

My heartstrings pull like taffy,
Each tug elicits laughter,
A tug-of-war with feelings,
I jest, at least I'm not frafter.

I trip on love, a comedic fall,
Like slipping on a banana peel,
Yet here I stand, proud and tall,
In the circus of life, I have appeal.

Cracks in the Armor

My armor shines, but it has flaws,
Like a knight who forgot to eat,
I battle on, despite the cause,
With crumbs on my breastplate, a quirky treat.

A sword of wit, my only shield,
I chuckle while I face the foe,
In this chaotic battlefield,
I jest, "Hey, look at that rainbow!"

Embracing the Storm

As clouds roll in, I greet the rain,
With open arms and silly grin,
I dance like no one sees my pain,
My wet socks squish, but I still spin.

Lightning strikes, oh what a show,
I mimic it with jazz hands bright,
In the downpour, I let it go,
Who knew I'd be the storm's delight?

Pathways of Endurance

Each step I take, a funny dance,
With every stumble, I lose my cool,
Yet here I am, taking the chance,
To trip through life, the world's my school.

And should I fall, I'll make it grand,
With somersaults and silly grins,
In this parade, hand in hand,
I'll laugh and say, 'Let the fun begin!'

A Tapestry of Trials

In the circus of my woes, I stand,
Juggling troubles with a clumsy hand.
Fell on my face, what a grand display,
Laughter echoes, brightens the gray.

Life's a slippery slope, what a ride,
I trip on my shoelaces, can't confide.
Each fall is a laugh, dressed in a frown,
Yet I wear my goof-ups like a crown.

A coffee spill, my brand-new shirt,
I wipe it off, with a grateful smirk.
Every mishap is a tale to spin,
Turning fumbles into grins within.

With bumps and bruises, I dance and twirl,
A comedy show in this crazy whirl.
So here's to mess-ups, my favorite splurge,
To living out loud, as I laugh and purge.

Awakened in the Aftermath

Early morning, I rise with a yawn,
Tripped on my cat, oh, how I brawn!
Tea goes flying, I nearly cry,
But there's humor in spills, oh my, oh my!

I wear a band-aid, a badge of pride,
A war with my toast, oh how I've tried.
Each charred bite is a lesson learned,
Toast may be burnt, but my humor is earned.

Life's little hiccups, I collect with glee,
Like socks with holes, they're a part of me.
I slip and I slide, what a slapstick scene,
Laughter my armor, keeping it clean.

With every mishap, I chuckle loud,
In the chaos of life, I'm too proud.
From slips on the floor to my wild hairdo,
I take on the challenges, and laugh with the view.

Wounds Untold

I tripped on my feet, oh what a sight,
My dignity scattered, lost in the night.
A bruise on my ego, a laugh in the air,
I'm just a mere dancer, without any flair.

With each awkward tumble, I rise with a grin,
Like a clown on my stage, I play for a win.
Each scrape tells a joke that I've come to embrace,
In the circus of life, I'm the funniest case.

My knees might be scraped, but my heart's still bright,
With band-aids of humor, I'll be alright.
I wear my missteps like a crown on my head,
Those wounds are just stories, where laughter is bred.

Shadows in the Light

Behind every giggle, a mishap may dwell,
Like a pie in the face, it's a tale to tell.
I stepped on a rake, it flipped with great grace,
Laughter erupted, oh what a wild race.

The clumsy parade of my daily affairs,
Is sprinkled with chuckles, and sometimes with glares.
For in all of these shadows, where mishaps reside,
A heart full of sparkle will always abide.

I dance with the shadows, they whisper my name,
In the light of the laughter, I'm never to blame.
So let the world chuckle at my silly plight,
For I find my way forward, in joy, not in fright.

The Beauty of Scars

The scar on my knee is a badge of the bold,
A war wound from childhood, a tale to be told.
I conquered the sandbox; I fought with great flair,
With a plastic toy sword and a brave, stubborn glare.

Each mark tells a story, a laugh in disguise,
From slip-ups on the ice to clumsy high-fives.
With every small scrape, I've learned to take flight,
Embracing the quirks that sparkle so bright.

I've painted my life with humorous stains,
Like badges of courage from my youthful campaigns.
There's beauty in turmoil, and joy in the scars,
So let's toast to laughter, beneath all the stars!

Mapping the Terrain of Hurt

I chart my mishaps like a treasure map,
With X marks the spot where I took a bad flap.
Each tumble's a story, a laugh long and loud,
I'm the jester of blunders, here's my proud crowd.

Navigating life's bumps with a smirk and a twirl,
Every downfall a dance, oh watch me unfurl.
In this cartography where pain meets delight,
I'll sketch out my laughter, as wrong feels so right.

With every new trip that I take on my way,
I'll gather these moments; they're here to stay.
So we'll plot this adventure, both silly and bright,
In the mapping of joy, I'll always take flight.

The Strength of Silent Tears

A drop of tear, a tussle in the night,
My pillow's soaked, it's a comedy in plight.
The jokes I tell, make shadows laugh,
While I'm wrestling with my half-sliced path.

Laughter echoes, among the midnight gripes,
In the circus of life, we juggle our types.
But who needs a clown when your heart's on a spree?
I'm the star of my show, oh what a decree!

Embracing the Storm

The clouds roll in with their thunderous roar,
I grab my umbrella, it's time to explore!
The rain might fall, but I'll dance in the midst,
While lightning's my spotlight, my daily twist.

Each puddle I jump is a splash of delight,
With my mismatched boots, I bounce left and right.
Laughing at thunder, I shout with cheer,
Who needs a spa day when the storm's here?

Heartbeats of Survival

With each heartbeat, I wiggle and squirm,
Life's a dance floor, a strange little term.
Got two left feet, but I'm finding my groove,
In this waltz of chaos, I'm starting to move.

When troubles are brewing like tea in a pot,
I sip on the humor, and give it a shot.
Life's a jigsaw, with pieces askew,
But laughter's the glue that pulls us on through!

Finding Solace in Suffering

In the depths of despair, there's a tickle of zest,
I trip on my thoughts, but I still feel blessed.
With a grin in the gloom, I'm the jester of fate,
Turning frowns into smiles, isn't life great?

Every mishap's a tale, spun with a twist,
Memories of chaos, oh, they can't be missed.
So I'll dance with my woes, in a comical cheer,
Finding solace in laughter, that's crystal clear!

Whispers of Resilience

If life gives you lemons, just wear a hat,
And squeeze those fruits while you dance like a cat.
Turn the frown upside down, with a simple grin,
For laughter's the secret to let joy in.

In puddles of sorrow, jump like a frog,
Hop away the blues, while you sing like a dog.
With bubbles of laughter, float high in the air,
Embrace silly moments, there's joy everywhere.

In Shadows We Grow

In the depths of the night, we trip on our feet,
Yet we roll like a tumbleweed, laughter's our beat.
Falling on faces, we laugh 'til we cry,
Shadows may chase us, but we'll still fly high.

With giggles for fuel and a wink for a start,
We wear our mishaps like a badge on our heart.
Finding light in the dark, we wiggle and sway,
In the shadows we grow, turning night into play.

Shattered but Unbroken

Like a plate that fell down, we scatter and shine,
A jigsaw of laughter, in pieces we align.
Cracks tell our story, in colors we beam,
Shattered yet silly, we're living the dream.

As we juggle our troubles, we dance in the rain,
Each slip brings a giggle, a chance to entertain.
With a hat made of hope and shoes full of cheer,
We're shattered but unbroken, let's give a loud cheer!

The Light Beneath the Struggle

There's a light under the bed, where the dust bunnies play,
They host little parties when we've had a long day.
With socks on our hands, we join in the fun,
For every dark corner, there's joy to be spun.

In the maze of our worries, we twirl and we shout,
Like a cereal box hero, we turn it all about.
With each quirk and each giggle, we climb every hill,
For beneath every struggle lies laughter, sweet thrill.

Breaths Amidst Chaos

In a kitchen, pot's on the blink,
Spaghetti gets a nod, perhaps a wink.
Chaos reigns, the cat runs by,
No one notices, not even I.

Mistaken salt for sugar today,
Baking pies, oops, on my way.
Laughter echoes, we stand and stare,
We found a smile hiding in despair.

Dishes tower, a building high,
Forks in battle, hear their sigh.
Yet we dance, a waltz divine,
In the whirlwind, we laugh and dine.

Life's a circus, clowns in line,
Falling flat, but we call it fine.
Wipe away tears with a cupcake's cream,
In this chaos, we find our dream.

The Lament of Lost Dreams

A kite once soared, now lost to trees,
Rope tangled up, can't catch the breeze.
Chasing memories like a wayward cat,
Each failed attempt, a comic prat.

Had plans to swim, but the pool was dry,
Diving for fortune, I barely try.
A paper boat capsized, oh dear me,
Yet here I float, on laughter's sea.

Had a dream to fly, now just a sprawl,
Glimmers of hope look like a ball.
With humor sharp as a sharpened pencil,
I sketch my fate, the lines so dense, though simple.

So raise a glass, let's toast tonight,
For every wrong turn, we'll make it right.
Lost dreams may stumble, but watch us dance,
In this mishmash, we still take a chance.

A Symphony of Struggles

With pots and pans, a clatter grand,
A symphony made with slapstick hand.
The dog's out howling a flat-note tune,
While we conduct chaos under the moon.

Mismatched socks, a sight to see,
Waltzing in style, just you and me.
Each trip and fall, a bumbling score,
Our lives, a concert of epic lore.

Coffee spills like a waterfall,
Stumbling through morning, we heed its call.
Yet we sing in tune with every mistake,
Our thoughts unite, like a large, loud quake.

In laughter's rhythm, we find our grace,
With every hiccup, we find our place.
Though struggles may try to steal our show,
We rock the stage, we steal the glow.

Threads Woven in Sorrow

Threads of color, tangled and bright,
We weave our woes with laughter's light.
Stitching together a patchwork quilt,
Of goofy fumbles and laughter built.

With each sad tale, we add a cheer,
Sewing mischief into every tear.
Laughing at woes, we dare to tread,
In each funny fiber, joy is spread.

A needle pokes, but oh the grin,
Who knew chaos could spark such win?
With every loop, we dance and spin,
Creating a tapestry where laughs begin.

So let the fabric of life parade,
In vibrant hues, our sorrows fade.
Threads woven tight, a quirky blend,
In this silly sorrow, our hearts mend.

Navigating the Storm

Waves keep crashing, what a sight,
I'm clinging tight with all my might.
Raindrops laugh, they think it's fun,
Splashing on me while I try to run.

Umbrellas fly like birds in glee,
Oh, how I wish they'd rescue me.
I slip and slide, a comedy,
Dance of a sailor, wild and free.

Thunder roars, but I just grin,
I'm swimming like a fish in sin.
Lightning's flashy, better than shows,
I just hope it doesn't strike my toes.

After the storm, I'll sip my tea,
Share the tales of my frolic spree.
Laughter's a boat, I float along,
Joking through life's wild, silly song.

Shards of Strength

Broken pieces everywhere,
I trip and tumble, what a scare!
But look, a gem shines in the mess,
I pick it up, I'm something, yes!

Duct tape dreams and super glue,
Hold me together, I'm a zoo!
With every slip, I laugh aloud,
I'm a warrior, kinda proud.

Laughter fuels my every crack,
I'm like a jigsaw with no back.
Each piece tells a story grand,
Of a silly, stubborn little band.

So here I stand, a quirky sight,
With shards of strength, I'll shine so bright.
Embracing chaos with a cheer,
Watch me sparkle, never fear!

The Dance of Perseverance

Stumbling steps on a sticky floor,
I twirl and whirl, wanting to soar.
The beat goes wild, it mocks my feet,
But watch me move, I can't be beat.

Falling flat like a pancake round,
I bounce back up without a sound.
Each awkward jig, a graceful fall,
I'm the life of the dance hall brawl.

Spinning left, then tripping right,
A dizzy dancer, what a sight!
But laughter lifts me from the ground,
In every stumble, joy is found.

So let's kick it, my wobbly crew,
We'll jive through life, just me and you.
With every misstep, I'll sing my song,
In this crazy dance, we all belong!

The Silent Symphony

Life's a tune played soft and sweet,
But I keep stepping on my feet.
Silence sings, and I can't hear,
The notes are missing, oh so dear!

Balloons deflate, what can I do?
I'll blow them up like a kangaroo!
A silent symphony turns to roar,
Every mishap just makes me want more.

In the quiet, I find delight,
Like a cat with a laser light.
Searching for rhythms in the void,
My silly antics can't be destroyed.

So here I hum my one-man show,
With laughter accompanying the flow.
In the silence, I'll dance and play,
Turning whispers into a bright ballet!

Silent Battles Waged

In the quiet, I trip on my shoes,
Making mishaps my daily news.
A dance of socks, a duel of cake,
Who knew that my breakfast could quake?

I laugh at my stumbles, it's how I thrive,
Each tumble's a joke, keeps me alive.
With bruises like badges, I strut with style,
A comedian's grace, it's all in the smile.

In the Depths of Despair

When the coffee spills and the toast won't pop,
I find myself laughing, oh, what a flop!
A cereal shower, a noodle parade,
In chaos, my laughter is finely displayed.

The missing keys just can't be found,
I check my pocket, then look around.
They're in the fridge! What a clever prank!
In the absurd, I feel full of spank.

Through the Fog of Heartache

Oh, love's sweet song, it can go so wrong,
Like socks in the dryer, it won't belong.
My heart takes a tumble, a slip on the floor,
Yet I grin wide, who could ask for more?

A heart that's bruised is still quite the show,
I juggle my feelings, but only for show.
With clowns in my heart and pranks on my sleeve,
In this circus of life, I still believe!

Born from the Fire

In the furnace of life, I stumble and roll,
Charred marshmallows crisp, but I'm on a stroll.
With ashes on my shirt and laughter in tow,
I come out a phoenix, just watch me glow.

Like spaghetti flung high on a wild dinner night,
My trials and errors are sheer comedic delight.
A warrior with humor, with scars that shine,
I dance with the flames, it's my punchline divine.

Beneath the Surface of Silence

In the quiet I often trip,
Stumble on my coffee sip.
Thoughts like squirrels dash about,
Chasing dreams I can't live without.

What's that noise, my mind aglow?
A distant laugh? Or just my toe?
Underneath this calm facade,
A circus rides in every nod.

Watch me grin through the bizarre,
Like a cat that's fallen from a car.
I dance alone, a jester's game,
Laughing loud in my own name.

Yet within this merry charade,
A hidden truth cannot evade.
Joy and chaos intertwine,
In silent depths, I redefine.

Lost in the Depths

I'm lost in thoughts without a clue,
Like socks that vanish, it's true.
Diving deep into my stew,
I find a fish that looks like you.

Beneath the bubbles of my mind,
Unicorns and munchkins combined.
Every swim becomes a splash,
In a sea of laughter, I dash.

Floating on my raft of jokes,
Dodging all the funny folks.
With every wave, a chuckle flows,
In depths where sanity never goes.

So here's my dance, a silly fling,
Wobbling like a new-born king.
Lost and found in depths profound,
With laughter as my life's rebound.

Seasons of Healing

Spring brings flowers, oh so bright,
Yet here I sneeze with all my might.
Pollen stings, but hey, it's fun,
Chasing rabbits in the sun.

Summer's heat, a blazing sphere,
Ice cream drips and kids' loud cheer.
In the shade, I take a nap,
Dreaming of a swan-shaped slap.

Autumn leaves swirl and twirl,
As I trip in my fancy whirl.
Pumpkin spice and jokes galore,
I laugh so hard, I hit the floor.

Winter's chill, the snowflakes dance,
In thermal socks, I take a chance.
Cocoa spills, a tasty mess,
In cozy warmth, I find success.

The Return to Self

Back to me, what a strange trip,
Like a penguin in a cruise ship.
Waddling on my own two feet,
In clown shoes, it's quite the feat.

Mirror, mirror, who's that guy?
With hair that looks like cotton candy high.
I pull a face, then burst out loud,
This laughter makes me feel so proud.

A little time, a little cheer,
I've found my heart, it feels so near.
In the circus of my jumbled mind,
Joy's the treasure that I find.

So here I stand, a joyful blast,
No more shadows of the past.
With every giggle, I reclaim,
The silly self, my brightest name.

Climbing Out of the Depths

I slipped on a banana peel,
But I found a way to feel.
With laughter as my best friend,
I'll rise up and ascend.

Each step is a silly dance,
Twisting like I'm in a trance.
The ground may hold its grip tight,
But I'll glow like a disco light.

My socks may not match today,
Yet I'll laugh and be okay.
Stumbling on a million dreams,
Who knew life had such funny themes?

So here I am, a jester proud,
Waving to the cheering crowd.
With laughter, I break the fall,
Life's a circus, after all!

Fragments of Hope

In a world of mixed-up hues,
I found joy in mismatched shoes.
Each step a music note that sings,
Life's a comedy with wild swings.

I tripped on my own two feet,
But the tumble was pretty sweet.
With giggles that come out like bells,
I embrace each minor hell.

A puzzle piece that doesn't fit,
Yet sparks a laugh when I sit.
Collecting chuckles like they're gold,
In every moment, courage bold.

Fragments sparkle, a quirky charm,
Turning chaos into calm.
With every blunder, light will grow,
Finding laughter in the low.

Burdens Transformed

My backpack's filled with rocks and cheese,
I carry them with silly ease.
Each chunk brings a hearty laugh,
Who knew burdens could be daft?

I juggle woes like circus clowns,
Bouncing highs and flopping downs.
Yet in the chaos, joy I find,
Transforming heaviness in kind.

The weight may sway, the straps may dig,
Yet I dance a goofy jig.
With every wobble, I let go,
Finding cheer in what I know.

So come, dear friend, let's pack it tight,
Laughing at our silly plight.
In burdens shared, we'll lift the weight,
Finding light in every fate!

A Journey Unraveled

I set off on this winding road,
Tripped over shoelaces in a load.
With a map that leads to nowhere fast,
I'll stay amused as I wander past.

The GPS is on the blink,
But I won't stop to overthink.
Each wrong turn brings a hearty cheer,
I'll pretend I'm on a treasure sphere.

With coffee stains and crumbs galore,
I'll make a picnic on the floor.
In every detour, giggles bloom,
The journey sparks from every room.

So let's toast to every slip,
And celebrate this funny trip.
For life's a ride, both wild and free,
Let's laugh along, you and me!

Rising from Ruins

I tripped on a stone, did a dance of dismay,
Got up with a grin, who needs pride anyway?
The ground may be hard, but my humor's a gem,
I laugh at the world, and it laughs back at them.

With scraped knees and stories that must be told,
I wore my mistakes like a coat made of gold.
Each tumble a lesson, each bruise a new friend,
In this circus called life, the show will not end.

The Space Between Joy

Happiness finds me in the oddest of places,
Like slipping on ice and making strange faces.
I wink at the sky with a comical flair,
In the space where joy lives, I'm a billionaire.

Sometimes I'm a clown, with a heart made of cheese,
Making the best of life's little unease.
When the going gets tough, and I miss the right cue,
I giggle at chaos—what else can I do?

Sails Against the Wind

My ship's caught a gust, but it's going off track,
I tightened the sails, yelled, "Bring the snack pack!"
With waves in my face and a grin ear to ear,
I sail through the struggle, fueled by good cheer.

The taller the waves, the higher I laugh,
In this wild ocean dance, I've found my path.
A pirate of jest, I navigate strife,
With a hearty 'Aye!' to the humor of life.

The Art of Endurance

In this marathon of madness, I trip, I spill,
But I bounce like rubber, oh, what a thrill!
Each footfall an echo of joy in disguise,
Endurance is laughter that never denies.

With every ache comes a joke, every pain brings a pun,
In the art of survival, oh what fun we run!
Through mazes of mishaps, I dance with a grin,
For the sweetest of victories start from within.

Castles Built on Sand

In a castle made of sand,
We play with dreams unplanned.
A wave comes in, it's not profound,
And suddenly, our home's unwound.

With buckets bright and spades in hand,
We laugh and build, it's all so grand.
But look! Here comes a seagull's flight,
And laughs at our soft, sandy plight.

Yet every grain and every laugh,
Is worth the awkward, silly path.
For what's a castle but a joke,
When the tide returns, and we just soak?

So we dance like fools on the shore,
While the sandcastle crumbles, forevermore.
And in this game, we've found our cheer,
For every loss brings laughter near.

The Heart's Resurgence

When my heart felt like a stone,
I wore my frown like a throne.
But hey, who knew laughter could swell,
And turn my misery into a spell?

With each chuckle, a crack appeared,
Releasing all that I once feared.
Like a balloon, I started to rise,
Witty remarks, my ultimate prize.

Now I don the crown of jest,
Turning disappointments into a fest.
Because a broken heart's not a mess,
When you add a splash of humor finesse.

So here's to rhythms of the heart,
Even when life feels torn apart.
With jokes and jests, we find our way,
Turning night into the funniest day.

Notes from the Edge

On the edge of reason's brink,
I scribble notes and dare to think.
Life's a circus, a silly play,
Where elephants wear tutus, hooray!

With every wobbly step I take,
My thoughts start flipping, like a flake.
I laugh at gravity, laugh at time,
Inventing chaos, creating rhyme.

Yet wisdom hides beneath the glee,
Even clowns know how to foresee.
A stumble here, a pratfall there,
Reminds us all, to breathe in air.

So I tip my hat to life's cheap tricks,
And dance around with all its flicks.
For every note from the edge I send,
Is a chance to find the humor's blend.

Seasons of Solitude

In winter's chill, I found my glee,
Wearing socks that don't match, just me!
Snowflakes fell like confetti bright,
As I danced around in sheer delight.

Spring blooms brought thyme for a giggle,
I'd trip on pollen, watch me wiggle.
With every sneeze and laugh I'd throw,
Nature's humor steals the show.

Summer's sun with blistering rays,
Made me invent plans for lazy days.
An iced tea spill? What a delight!
Laughter echoed in the sheer sunlight.

When autumn comes with leaves to crunch,
I'll hug my cat and munch a lunch.
For solitude is a silly game,
In every season, I find the same.

Rising from Ashes

I tripped on my dreams, face full of dust,
Yet here I am laughing, in humor I trust.
I rise up like a phoenix, though it's quite absurd,
With wings made of band-aids, and hopes slightly blurred.

I spilled my hot coffee, burnt edges and fate,
Yet I dance on the ruins, I cannot be late.
My heart's on a roller coaster, laughter's the ride,
With every mishap, I'm joyfully fried.

Unspoken Wounds

I wear my charades like a professional mime,
Silent but funny, it's a comical crime.
With sarcasm handy and a jest in my heart,
I mask these odd stitches; it's really an art.

My scars tell a story, but humor's the key,
I laugh at the chaos, it sometimes suits me.
I juggle my troubles; they're just silly clowns,
With each little stumble, I wear laughter's crown.

Echoes of Resilience

I'm an echo of giggles, a riddle in strife,
Dodging life's curveballs with a fork and a knife.
I aim for the belly laughs, skip over the gloom,
Finding joy in the chaos, I dance in my room.

Each stumble a giggle, each trip is a jest,
Wounds heal through chuckles; oh, isn't life blessed?
I'm tackling my shadows, one pun at a time,
With a wink and a grin, I all but rhyme.

Silent Battles

In the arena of silence, I hear echoes snort,
Wrestling my worries with laughter's report.
I might have some bruises, but they're badges of fun,
Each laugh a small victory, I've already won.

With a snicker and snort, I face off with fear,
My silent skirmish, with punchlines so clear.
I juggle my thoughts, like a clown on the way,
In the circus of life, I'm here for the play.

When the Heart Breaks Open

Oh, did my heart just crack?
I thought it was a snack!
Silly me, I'm in a stew,
Where's my cake and ice cream too?

I check for glue, it's gone for good,
Tried to mend it with some wood!
Now it beats with a squeaky sound,
Looks like I've lost the love I found.

It's a comedy, this heart of mine,
Like a joke without a punchline.
Yet I'm laughing as I trip,
Maybe I just need a dip!

So bring your best repair kit here,
With band-aids and goofy cheer.
When hearts break, it's quite a sight,
Let's laugh about it, it's alright!

The Strength of Brokenness

Like a vase that's missed the shelf,
I'll patch it up with hope myself.
Duct tape's a hero in disguise,
Holding all my happy lies.

Wobbling on this crumbled floor,
I laugh till I can't take much more.
The strength I find in shattered fragments,
Only boosts my chuckle magnets.

With jagged edges, I still shine bright,
Like a quirky disco ball at night.
Every crack a tale to tell,
Of momentary slips, oh well!

Embrace the mess, let's have a dance,
With broken pieces, take a chance.
In misfit forms, we find our way,
And giggle through the wild display.

Where Darkness Meets Dawn

In the gloom, I trip and fall,
Where's that light? I hear a call!
I fumble around, what a fright,
But hey, I see the morning light!

With bedhead wild, I look a mess,
In darkness, I just confess.
Bumping walls and laughing loud,
I'm in my own comedy crowd.

Every step's a wobbly dance,
I might as well enhance my chance!
Lost in shadows, but oh, what fun,
I'll caffeinate with a silly pun.

So, here's to dawn and giggles bright,
Where laughter finds you in the night.
Through every stumble, hear my cheer,
The day is here! The joke is clear!

Tides of Turmoil

Riding waves of chaos, a sight to behold,
Surfing on emotions, some sassy, some bold.
Splashing through the storm, I dance with a grin,
Who knew turmoil could bring such a spin?

Like a rubber ducky lost in the sea,
I bob and weave, oh, woe is me!
Navigating whirlpools of silly despair,
With a clown nose on, I'm ready to dare!

Each tide brings laughter, it lifts me up high,
Every crash of the wave makes me wry.
I roll with the punches, bouncing just right,
Who knew turmoil could be such a delight?

So here's to splashes and bubbly glee,
When life gets wavy, remember to see.
Through each twist and turn, find your cheer,
In the tides of chaos, I'm still here!

Dances with Shadows

In a room full of gloom, I took to the floor,
Tripping on toes, what a laugh, and more!
The shadows joined in, what a silly sight,
We tangoed through twilight, oh what pure delight!

Fell flat on my face, but with flair and a grin,
The shadows roared laughter; it just had to win.
I waggled my arms like a chicken in flight,
They mimicked my moves; what a sweet little fright!

Twisted and twirled, like a noodle in soup,
Shadows chuckled softly, joining the troop.
We spun into laughter, what a glorious mess,
In this gloomy old room, we felt truly blessed!

And as the night waned, right into the dawn,
Me and my shadows, we bobbed on the lawn.
With each silly stumble, I found joy anew,
In the dance of the dark, I became light too!

Crafting Light from Gloom

Under the clouds, I would gather some cheer,
Mixing laughter and giggles like a weird engineer.
With a sprinkle of funny and a dash of jest,
I paint the gray skies with the joy quite blessed!

I took a gray spoon and I stirred it around,
Making sunshine out of each quirky sound.
An umbrella with holes and some lemony zest,
Served up giggles, yes, it's truly the best!

A backwards umbrella, oh what a fine line,
Catching the chuckles, just a matter of time.
In the face of the gloom, I threw a grand feast,
And invited my worries, but they never increased.

From darkness, I'll shape all things funny and bright,
Crafting each moment, transforming the night.
So when life hands you gloom with a side of despair,
Just twist it, and laugh, and show it you care!

The Resilient Heart

With a heart made of rubber, I bounced right back,
Hopping over troubles on my happy track.
Life threw me curveballs with a side of a joke,
But I just laughed louder till my spirit awoke!

I wore a heart hat; it protected my glee,
While jiving on rhythms, oh what a sight to see!
Each thump, each giggle, a new beat would start,
In this funny old dance, I became my own art.

Facing life's challenges with a jester's delight,
Dancing through sorrows like a star in the night.
I stitched joy into seams of my weary attire,
And warmed up the cold with my heart's little fire!

My heart may be tender, but it's silly and raw,
Bouncing through hardships with a merry guffaw.
So here's to the heart that won't fall apart,
In the laughter of life, I'll always take part!

Climbing the Walls of Woe

Scaling my worries like a wall made of cheese,
It wobbled and giggled, bringing me to my knees.
I sprouted some wings with my laughter to soar,
Who knew that my troubles would offer such lore?

I clambered on up with a pop and a squeak,
The wall gave a chuckle, which made me feel weak.
It tickled my tummy as I flew ever high,
The woes made me giggle like a kite in the sky!

Each brick was a story, each crack held a jest,
With a shrug and a grin, I'd conquer the rest.
If I slip and I fall, I'll just bounce back again,
Life's just a game, and I'm here to pretend!

So here's to the climbs, and the laughter it brings,
Let's shimmy and shake under this wall made of flings.
In climbing my sorrows, I learned something grand,
There's joy to be found, just reach for its hand!

Reflections in the Ruins

In a world where chaos reigns,
I trip on bricks and avoid the stains.
With laughter echoing in the sky,
I juggle my worries, oh my, oh my!

In the wreckage, I find my cheer,
Cracked mirrors reflect what's near.
Dancing shadows, a comic play,
Lost my map, but hey, it's okay!

Sipping tea from a rusty cup,
Build a throne from the growing up.
Broken dreams, a funny sight,
I wear my scars like a clown's delight.

So here's to life's spectacular show,
Falling down in style, let it flow.
Amidst the ruins, I shall prance,
With humor's grace, I take my chance.

The Weight We Carry

I waddle 'neath this heavy load,
Like a turtle on a bumpy road.
Life's packing peanuts, they make me trip,
But I'll strut my stuff, take a goofy dip.

My back is bent, but my spirit's grand,
Like a penguin trying to make a stand.
With every sigh, I craft a joke,
Who knew burdens could make us poke?

Carrying dreams on the public bus,
I laugh as people glance at us.
With giggles and gripes, we'll navigate,
And turn our weight into first-rate fate.

So come collect your bag of woes,
We'll trade in laughter, that's how it goes.
Each burden shared is a lighter load,
So let's walk this hilarious road.

From Desolation to Determination

In this wasteland, what do we find?
A treasure map that's misaligned.
With a compass that spins and a map that's torn,
I'll laugh while finding the place I was born.

Battles fought in pajamas bold,
With snacks at hand, I reclaim my gold.
No victory dance, just a funny jig,
Who knew success would look like a pig?

I stumble on hopes, a leaky boat,
But I'll sail on laughter, keep me afloat.
Let's paint the town with colors divine,
From ashes to triumph, a wacky design.

So here's to grit with a splash of fun,
We're laughing hard, we've already won.
With each smile, I'll conquer the fate,
The road to success may just be first-rate.

Grief in the Garden

In a patch where weeds grow tall,
I plant my sorrows, hope they don't sprawl.
Compost my tears, sprinkle them light,
Buried in laughter, they might take flight.

The flowers bloom with a crooked grin,
They dance in shadows, where laughs begin.
Each petal holds a giggle or two,
In this garden, my joys are due.

With gnomes that wink and trees that sway,
I talk to daisies, they know the way.
We harvest smiles from the soil deep,
Overgrown troubles, we choose to leap.

Among the thorns, I find my place,
With humor's arm, I embrace the space.
In grief's garden, I plant my cheer,
Watch my joy bloom, year after year.

Whispered Resilience

In the shadows where laughter hides,
I trip on dreams, oh how life rides.
With a grin, I stumble 'round,
Making joy in this circus town.

A banana peel is my best friend,
With each slip, the giggles blend.
I wear my woes like a silly hat,
Turning frowns to a playful spat.

Chasing rainbows, I trip and twirl,
While my worries dance in a whirl.
The world may frown, but here I stand,
With laughter as my guiding hand.

Oh, the stories that we'll unfold,
Witty tales made of silver and gold.
In the chaos, we will shine,
With a wink and a cheesy line.

Counting the Stars in Darkness

In the midnight sky, I find my spark,
Counting stars while I trip in the dark.
They twinkle at me, a cosmic cheer,
Reminding me to face my fear.

I once bumped heads with a comet's tail,
Now I giggle at my epic fail.
When hope seems lost, I'll dance in glee,
Making constellations out of me!

I wear a cape made from bedsheets fine,
Zooming around, feeling divine.
Each stumble a step in this comedy,
Finding joy in every oddity.

So in the dark, I'll keep my score,
Laughing loud, who could ask for more?
With stars for friends, I brave the night,
Chasing dreams, oh what a sight!

A Journey Through Shadows

In the land where shadows prance,
I trip on rocks, but still I dance.
Whispers of humor fill the air,
With every fall, I learn to care.

My feet may stumble, my heart will soar,
Every mishap opens a door.
I juggle my fears like a clown on stage,
Turning struggles into a laughing page.

The shadows giggle with me at play,
As I learn to dance my worries away.
With a broomstick horse, I ride the tide,
In this crazy journey, I won't hide.

So here's to the leaps that make us trip,
In this shadow dance, let laughter rip.
With each wild flip, I'll smile and sing,
Finding joy in everything.

The Echo of Endurance

In the echoes of my silly plight,
I slip on laughter, oh what a sight!
With giggles bouncing from wall to wall,
I find my strength whenever I fall.

Life's a comedy, a topsy-turvy show,
Where woes become punchlines in a row.
As I trip and tumble, I strike a pose,
Turning troubles to winks and smiles that glow.

Every echo tells a story bright,
Of foolish falls that feel just right.
In the chaos, we create a tune,
A symphony of joy beneath the moon.

So listen closely to the fun that rings,
In the dance of life, we embrace the flings.
With a chuckle loud, I bravely steer,
In this echo, joy is always near.

Echoes of Endurance

With socks mismatched, I stride along,
My coffee spilled, it feels so wrong.
Yet laughter bubbles, through my plight,
I'll dance in mud, oh what a sight!

A flat tire here, a shoe that's stuck,
I trip on air, oh what's my luck?
I wear my bruises like a badge,
In every stumble, I find a laugh!

The cat ran off with my lunch today,
I chase it down, in a clumsy play.
With every mishap, there's joy to chase,
In life's big circus, I find my place!

So here's to the rides, the bumpy paths,
I'll keep my smile, despite the gaffes.
With every laugh, the heart will mend,
These wacky tales will never end!

A Symphony of Healing

Dancing to tunes of pots and pans,
The cat joins in, with awkward plans.
My cooking skills? A comedy show,
Smoke alarms sing, oh what a woe!

With each small cut, I learn to jest,
Like playing doctor in my own quest.
Band-aids here, and laughs all around,
Who knew healing could be so profound?

The gym's a trap, oh what a joke,
Weights like bricks, I nearly choke.
Yet, seeing others tumble too,
Brings giggles out, just like new!

So let's compose this playful tune,
With silly steps, we'll chase the moon.
Laughter heals the wounds we bear,
In this symphony, we breathe fresh air!

Rising from Ashes

A toast to falls, and tumbles grand,
I trip on toes, just as I planned!
Yet as I rise, with grace anew,
I laugh aloud, oh look at you!

From burnt toast to soggy fries,
I wear my flaws like a bright disguise.
With confidence that won't back down,
I'll wear my clumsiness like a crown!

Candle wax drips, what a delight,
I've lit my home like it's nightlight.
In every mess, a story grows,
Of silly dreams and pesky woes!

So let the ashes fall where they may,
I'll scoop them up in a jokester's play.
From what seems lost, I find my flair,
In every blunder, joy is there!

Unfurling from Darkness

In the depths of night, I lose my keys,
I search like mad, my thoughts a breeze.
Yet shadows whisper, with a grin,
It's just a game; where have you been?

With every hiccup, I find the light,
Behind each stumble, joy's in sight.
A dance of shadows, a jig of fun,
Who knew I could be on the run?

From coffee stains to mismatched socks,
Each day unfolds with funny knocks.
The darkness hums a jolly tune,
As I embrace the quirks of June!

So here's to mishaps, let laughter reign,
From tangled thoughts to silly pain.
With every misstep, a hearty cheer,
Unfurling brightly, without a fear!

Beyond the Veil of Sorrow

Beneath the cloud, a dance we share,
With slip-ups and laughter in the air.
We trip on life like kids at play,
Each tumble brings a smile our way.

A pie in the sky, the world a stage,
We juggle our woes with some comic rage.
Tears mix with giggles as we unwind,
Life's little mishaps, a treasure to find.

Through jest and jive, we spin our tale,
Lost in the punchlines, we never pale.
Puppies in bow ties, what a delight,
Laughter blooms even in the night.

So here's to the cheer in the midst of strife,
A wink and a nod, oh what a life!
With hiccups and chuckles, we'll always prevail,
Beyond the veil, our spirits won't fail.

Contrasts of Closure

When life hands you lemons, just make a pie,
Add a sprinkle of joy, let your laughter fly.
For every dark cloud that looms in the sky,
A rainbow of humor is always nearby.

We dance with our shadows, give them a name,
Invite them to parties, it's part of the game.
With each awkward moment, we all chuckle bright,
Turn woes into punchlines, what a silly sight!

A pun here, a giggle, we master the art,
Finding the funny is where we all start.
So raise your glass high for the laughter we share,
In the waltz of our troubles, we've no room for despair.

At times we may stumble, but who really cares?
With jokes on our lips, we're light as the air.
So here's to the laughter that sparks every day,
In the contrasts we face, we'll smile either way.

Resilience Under Pressure

When life goes haywire, we roll with a grin,
Spaghetti on the walls? Let the pasta begin!
We juggle our chaos with flair and some cheer,
Turning frowns to giggles, oh my, what a year!

With duct tape and dreams, we patch up our soul,
Crafting mishaps into a comical bowl.
We slip and we slide, yet still find our beat,
It's a dance of resilience, so light on our feet.

For every still moment, a chuckle we'll conjure,
In the messiness of life, never let it ponder.
A tickle here, a wink to the side,
We'll embrace all the flashes, our joyful ride.

So toast to our spirit, our quirky parade,
With laughter as armor, we'll never just fade.
Each pratfall a chapter, a jest that we share,
In the circus of life, let's dance without care.

Through the Veil of Grief

In shadows we giggle, our hearts sometimes ache,
But we find silly tales in every heartache.
When tears fall like rain, we break out the snacks,
In a comedy show, we'll patch up the cracks.

With socks on our hands and a dance in the aisle,
We flirt with our sorrows, and manage a smile.
For life's but a jest, a laugh if you dare,
Wrap up the woes in a big teddy bear.

We treat every teardrop like confetti of old,
Craft stories that shimmer, both tender and bold.
A wink to the past, we embrace our strange paths,
Join in the fun, let's make room for our laughs.

So raise up your voices, let laughter abound,
In the echoes of joy, new hope will be found.
For beyond every heartache lies humor, it's true,
In the veil of what's hard, we make our debut!

Threads of Courage

In the closet of my heart, I search for threads,
Stitching up laughter, avoiding heavy leads.
With needle and humor, I poke at the dark,
Finding joy in the jabs, igniting a spark.

Behind every frown, there's a joke to reveal,
Like rubber chickens, our woes can squeal.
With every lost sock, another tale unfolds,
In the tapestry of life, we're just being bold.

Oh, the riptide of mishaps, it pulls at my shoe,
Yet I dance in the waves, like I'm at a zoo.
When the laundry gets tangled, and laughter escapes,
I wear my mishaps like colorful capes.

So, here's to the stitches that hold us all tight,
Dancing through chaos, we'll be alright.
With courage in stitches, and humor at hand,
We'll sew up our lives, in this quirky land.

Beneath the Weight of Wounds

Underneath my backpack, there lies a great load,
With snacks and bad puns, on this humor road.
I walk with a limp, but I toss out a quip,
While balancing laughter, like a circus trip.

My past is a clumsy parade of mishaps,
Yet underneath each trip, I find some new snaps.
With every misstep, a joke slips on by,
Like a banana peel's dance, beneath the blue sky.

The weight of the world may have me in tow,
But I trip on my laughter, and still make the show.
With a chuckle I carry my wounds as my friends,
In the circus we call life, the humor just blends.

So here's to the bruises that teach us to laugh,
Turning sorrow to jokes, let's enjoy the craft.
With silly balloons, let's float all day long,
Beneath heavy burdens, we pretend we're so strong.

Blossoms from Thorns

From the prickly patches, new blooms will arise,
With a giggle or two, as my swan song belies.
Petals wrapped in laughter, they dance in the breeze,
While the thorns crack a smile, oh, what a tease!

When I trip on a thorn, I'll whisper out 'ouch',
But tuck in a laugh, like a cozy old couch.
With a bouquet of Guffaws, I'm ready to roam,
In a garden of giggles, I feel right at home.

Oh, the humor in struggles, it's ripe for the pick,
In the thicket of chaos, I find my own trick.
With every sharp jab, comes a punchline so bright,
Colorful blooms, giggling under the light.

So here's to the blossoms that give us a grin,
Turning each thorn into laughter within.
In our quirky bouquet, let's dance with delight,
Sprouting joy from the thorns, under the moonlight.

Navigating Turbulent Seas

Sailing through waves with a smile on my face,
My ship's got a squeak, what a comical pace!
With wind in my sails, I'm off on a spree,
Turning storms into giggles, what a sight to see.

The compass spins wildly, like my head full of jest,
But I find my horizon, laughing is best.
With each bumpy gallivant, a sea shanty's born,
I'm a captain of chuckles, through sun and through scorn.

When the waves crash and roll, I just dance on the deck,
Pretending I'm swimming, I might get a check.
With sea monsters grinning, I'm navigating right,
In this turbulent journey, I'll giggle till night.

So let's hoist the sails, and embrace the wild ride,
Through tempest and tickles, I'll grin, full of pride.
With cannonballs of laughter, I'll sail to the end,
Navigating life's ripples, with joy as my friend.

The Unseen Journey

In socks too tight, I take a stride,
My coffee spills, I need a guide.
But laughter comes, a jolly friend,
Who shares a joke, the chaos bends.

With every trip, I take a fall,
The world so big, I feel so small.
Yet in the slip, there's joy's embrace,
Life's circus act, a funny race.

I dance with awkward, wobbly feet,
The clumsy turns, a silly feat.
Beneath mishaps, a treasure shines,
In giggles shared, the heart entwines.

So here I stand, in silly woe,
A clown in life's grand, funny show.
With every blooper, cheers abound,
In invisible paths, joy is found.

Foundations of Fortitude

Upon a stool, one leg is shy,
I wobble forth, a daring try.
The pizza box, my throne of dreams,
I grapple with my silly schemes.

In every wobble, there's a grin,
A dance of effort, let's begin!
The peanut butter on my nose,
Reminds me how pure humor grows.

With life's weird tricks, I often trip,
Yet laughter's here; it's not a blip.
The joyous falls we come to share,
Create a bond beyond compare.

So when I build with mismatched bricks,
I find it's all a set of tricks.
Foundations deep, with laughter's dust,
In brave folly, we surely trust.

Unraveling the Heavy Threads

My sweater shrinks, it's now a vest,
But still I wear it, I'm the best.
The tangled yarns of life's design,
A comedy of loss, divine.

With every knot, a giggle gleams,
In chaos sewn, we weave our dreams.
The socks unmatched, a style unique,
A fashion show, so bold, so chic.

Unraveling woes, a playful strife,
In twisting threads, we find our life.
A quilt of mischief, stitched with care,
In every patch, jokes fill the air.

So here we stand, with threads of cheer,
In tangled laughs, we persevere.
With humor's thread, we're bound so tight,
In droplets of joy, we find our light.

Beneath Life's Crust

Beneath the crust of daily grind,
Lies hidden gold, it's quite the find.
A burnt toast laugh, a breakfast win,
In charred delights, we dive right in.

In life's flaky layers, joy does bloom,
A chocolate chip in every room.
The dough may rise with heavy weight,
But laughter lightens every plate.

Beneath the surface, pies may crack,
Yet in each slice, there's no lack.
For friendship's sprinkle, sweet and bright,
Turns every bite into sheer delight.

So here we stand, with crumbs to share,
In every pastry, love and care.
Beneath the crust, our hearts, they leap,
In bites of joy, our laughter keeps.

Beyond the Veil of Hurt

When life hands you lemons, make some pie,
Squeeze a bit of laughter, let it fly.
A band-aid on a heart, or a silly grin,
Sometimes the best humor is where we begin.

So grab a rubber chicken, wear it with pride,
Dance like nobody's watching, toss worries aside.
For every bruise and every scrape,
There's always room for a slapstick escape.

With jokes as our armor, we'll take a stand,
Giggling 'til we're dizzy, that's the plan.
No frowns allowed, let the chuckles unfold,
Laughter's the story that never grows old.

Behind every tear lies a tickle or two,
So tell me a pun, come on, make it a few!
For even in darkness, when gloom's at the helm,
A hearty laugh helps to create our own realm.

Cracks in the Armor

My armor's a bit rusty, it squeaks when I move,
Got dents from life's battles, but hey, that's the groove.
With each little crack, there's a story to share,
Laughter's the polish that shows that I care.

I trip over feelings and stumble on style,
With mismatched socks making me smile.
Each clumsy misstep is a dance of delight,
Who needs perfect when you've got giggles in sight?

A helmet of humor, I'll wear it with pride,
Wobbling through life as the chuckles collide.
For every bruise is just proof that I try,
And laughter's the wind that lifts me to fly.

So here's to the flaws that make us unique,
Embrace every quirk, let your laughter peak.
In cracks of our armor, true beauty can gleam,
With laughter and madness, we'll live out our dream.

A Journey to the Horizon

Setting sail with giggles, I'm ready to roam,
A horizon of humor, my steadfast home.
With calamitous laughter as my trusty guide,
I'll ride the tide of chaos, let waves collide.

Maps drawn in crayons, no compass in sight,
But with joy as my captain, I'm feeling just right.
Every bump on the road is a dance we can share,
Twisting and turning with a grin laid bare.

So bring on the storms, I'll dive headfirst in,
With a snorkel of giggles and silly whim.
The waves might be wavy, the wind might howel,
Yet laughter's the lifeboat, I'll never scowl.

Together we journey, through valleys and peaks,
With mischief and madness, it's laughter that speaks.
When troubles arise, let them come as they may,
With joy as my paddle, I'll drift far away.

The Beauty of Brokenness

In shards and in pieces, we're still quite divine,
Cracked pots can still hold the best vintage wine.
With winks and with giggles, our flaws spark delight,
A bouquet of laughter, our hearts take flight.

Embrace all your quirks, let them shine like a star,
For every misstep leads you to who you are.
A blunder, a malady, a trip or a fall,
Just fuel for the laughs, let's break down the wall.

With silly mishaps, we're all just a team,
Painting our lives with a whimsical dream.
For in every fracture, there's beauty combined,
A tapestry woven, uniquely designed.

So here's to the mess, to the giggles we share,
For every mishap brings us closer, I swear.
In the beauty of brokenness, laughter will glow,
Let's dance through the chaos, allow the joy to flow.

Roots of Fortitude

In the garden where we fall,
Laughter echoes, a hearty call.
Worn-out shoes and tangled weeds,
Stronger still, from broken seeds.

Cracked sidewalks that twist and bend,
Each bruise a joke, a funny trend.
We trip and giggle, that's our way,
Roots will wiggle, come what may.

Beneath the dirt, we plant our dreams,
With every laugh, the sunlight beams.
A quirky dance, a wobble and sway,
In silly steps, we find our play.

So when the world feels like a mess,
We joke, we grin, we wear our stress.
With humor as our trusty guide,
We grow in laughter, side by side.

Rebirth in the Ruins

In crumbled walls, we find our spark,
With rubber chickens, we make our mark.
Each flake of paint, a story told,
Of clowning hearts, defying cold.

The bricks may crack, the roof might leak,
But laughter's language is what we speak.
We juggle dreams amidst the dust,
Finding joy in all we trust.

With sippy cups of silly cheer,
We toast to faults, we've nothing to fear.
From ruins bright, new life will bloom,
Humor's light dispels the gloom.

So here's to mess, to all that's wild,
In cosmic jest, we're nature's child.
Rebirth in ruins, the fun doesn't cease,
We find our joy, our sweet release.

Shadows Beneath the Surface

In shadows where the giggles dwell,
Whispers of fun begin to swell.
The monsters there may look quite grim,
But make them dance on a whim!

A shadow puppet's silly face,
Wobbling 'round with giddy grace.
We chuckle at the deepest fears,
With every laugh, we drown the tears.

So when the light begins to dim,
We spark our joy, the hum and whim.
Beneath the surface, laughter's found,
And silly shadows bounce around.

Let's paint the dark with bursts of light,
In every giggle, we'll take flight.
So bring your quirks and join the game,
In shadowed depths, we'll never shame.

The Heaviness of Healing

With bandaids stuck on every scar,
We laugh at life, our silly star.
In healing pain, a weight we bear,
Yet jokes and jests fill up the air.

Like turtles in a marathon race,
We stumble on with an awkward grace.
Each quirky step, a tale to tell,
Silly songs turn wounds to swell.

We trudge through mud in powdery shoes,
Finding humor in every bruise.
When life feels heavy, we won't recline,
We'll dance like goofballs, and that's just fine.

So here's to laughs in sticky times,
Where giggles bloom in broken rhymes.
With every chuckle, we rise anew,
In the heaviness, we find our crew.

Threads of Light

In the dark, there's a shimmer, a spark,
Like a cat in a hat, trying to leave its mark.
Juggling socks while riding a bike,
Laughter blooms in moments we strike.

We trip on our shoes and dance with a grin,
Stumbling through life, where to begin?
A pie in the face, oh what a sight,
Chasing our woes with sheer delight.

With each step we take, there's a twist and a twirl,
Finding joy in the chaos, a laugh or a whirl.
Cupcakes on heads and laughter so bright,
In every hiccup, there's warmth and light.

So let's wear our hearts like oversized shoes,
And bask in the giggles; it's a win if we choose.
For even in shadows, a tickle might bloom,
Turning gloom into giggles, brightening the room.

Navigating the Abyss

In the ocean of trials, I started to float,
With a rubber ducky, don't you dare gloat.
Kicking and splashing, I swim like a fool,
Riding the waves, just breaking the rule.

Lost in a whirlpool, I grab at some cheese,
Not exactly the rescue, but still, it could please.
Bubbles of laughter popping in space,
Why worry their roars when you can smile with grace?

I wave to the fish, who wear monocle eyes,
While they judge my shark swim, I'm donned in disguise.
A snorkel of goofiness aids my descent,
Sinking in laughter, I'm perfectly bent.

So down in the abyss, I twirl like a pro,
Chasing the currents, I giggle, "Let's go!"
For every dive deep can come with a jest,
Dancing on troubles, I wear my best vest.

Beneath the Weight

Carrying burdens like a pack of bricks,
I trip over thoughts, doing silly tricks.
A walrus in waders, oh, watch me slip,
Falling in laughter, just need a quick grip.

With each heavy sigh, I leap like a frog,
Jumping to conclusions like a confused dog.
My backpack's a monster that growls with disdain,
Yet inside is a tickle that dances in rain.

I'm juggling my sorrows like popcorn afloat,
Dropping kernels of joy in my oversized coat.
Every stumble brings chuckles, oh what a sight,
For crushing my worries brings delight in the night.

Beneath every weight, a joke finds its space,
Wrapping woes in giggles, I'm winning the race.
So let's hoist our load with a wink and a grin,
For laughter's the remedy, let the fun begin.

The Other Side of Sorrow

Would you believe me if I said it's a hoot?
On the other side of gloom, there's a musical flute.
Sorrow's just sitting, waiting to play,
But brings in a drummer who laughs all the way.

An umbrella of giggles shields all rainy days,
While wiggles and wobbles lead laughter astray.
I'm chasing the shadows with pies in my hands,
Finding joy in the slips as my humor expands.

Behind every tear, there's a punchline in waiting,
Like ducks in a row, at a fair celebrating.
The bakery's open for a cupcake affair,
With sprinkles of humor floating in the air.

So dance through the drizzle, twirl under the sun,
Laughter's a treasure; let's not overrun.
For past every sorrow lies bright, joyful peaks,
With giggles and grins, it's the laughter that speaks.